JOHN PAUL II

Title of the Polish original
Jan Pawel II
© 1990 Parol Company, Krakow

Published in 1992 by Ignatius Press, San Francisco
© 1992 Barbara Wasowski and Niki Hauke
All rights reserved
ISBN 0–89870–424–3 (HB)
0–89870–421–9 (SB)
Library of Congress catalogue number 92–71934
Printed in Hong Kong

JOHN PAUL II

ADAM BUJAK

Foreword by
Andrzej Wajda

John Paul II—this is the name we find on the front cover. This publication sets before itself a brave goal: it aims at facilitating our encounter with the only person in history who bears that name.

Just as his Wadowice home, which is open to visitors, allows us to get a glimpse of the childhood and adolescent years of the Holy Father, this album attempts to bring to light the environment within which the Saint Peter of our times now lives.

May the Lord bless the author of this work and all those who receive it!

Cardinal Franciszek Macharski
Metropolitan Archbishop of Krakow

Can I resist looking at these photographs through the prism of a film director who has spent his life searching for the mystery of truth in actors' faces? Although the person of John Paul II provokes in us Poles particularly strong emotions, I wanted to come a little bit closer to the mystery I perceive when leafing through this album by looking at the pictures from the perspective of my own experience.

The eyes of the entire world are riveted to the person who provided the inspiration for these photographs. But John Paul II achieves something more—in his public appearances he concentrates the mind of everyone who approaches him. He makes every moment of his contact with people meaningful and unique. Even the practiced eye of a film director cannot trace in his face the slightest inkling of unconcern or impatience, which would seem natural and unavoidable.

Can such concentration be explained by self-discipline alone, by full control of a body trained to function in ascetic conditions? John Paul II was once asked why in his Polish years he greeted the faithful only by stretching his arms forward, and now he spreads them apart in his famous gesture. "I have more to embrace now!"

This simple and amazing answer is probably hidden in every gesture seen in these photographs.

In order to find out what lies behind this intense concentration, which makes other faces look hazy and unfocused, I have to delve deeper. Whether he carries the Cross in the Colosseum, following the path of the first martyrs, or kisses the ground to begin one of his pastoral visits, or talks to children or to the sick, John Paul II acts in full conviction that what is happening at a given moment must be brought to complete fulfillment.

For the image of truth that we see in these pictures to achieve such a strong expression, two powerful forces must be at work:

> Awareness of who I am
> and a clear sense of where I am going.

No outward trappings brought about by self-confidence, extensive practice, or composure can produce this strong effect, which is renewed at every contact with another person. This is why John Paul II's face is at once so vivid and so peaceful.

This is why people the world over see in his face not only the symbol of the leader of Christianity, but they glimpse in it the testimony of truth and awareness of purpose—they see *the face of man*.

What about the impressions of an artist, an author, a photographer, which this face produces?

I myself am surprised, but these pictures give me the irresistible impression that "no photographer was present at their conception". He stepped back with his skills, ingenuity, and artistic preconceptions and gave the floor to what silently speaks from the pages of this album: the face of the man who has the largest number of responsibilities of all people but is never in a hurry.

It is not Adam Bujak who guides his camera, it is the power of John Paul II's personality that enforces discipline and distance on the lens. The photographer simply knew how to fit into this situation, and may he be praised for that.

Leafing through the final pages of the album, I get the feeling that I am missing something that I and all those who have had the privilege of meeting John Paul II in person have experienced—his strong and unique handshake.

But no artistic device can render the flavor of that experience.

Andrzej Wajda
Jerusalem, March 27, 1988

The day of October 16, 1978, was for me very special, because I had been documenting the life of Bishop, Archbishop, and Cardinal Karol Wojtyla for several years. On this memorable day, we all started running wild with joy. Half of the population of Krakow, maybe more, came out into the streets. Even on entering a store, people would shout with joy: Cardinal Wojtyla is pope! Young people were dancing and singing in large groups. I even saw dancing priests and nuns. But amidst this elation I recognized that someone very close to me was leaving. I recalled his Christmas greetings, postcards he had sent me, and those very bracing and uplifting meetings with him.

When young Karol Wojtyla moved into a house on Tyniecka Street with his father (I could see the house from the window of my apartment), he often passed by my place. It would appear that I, then only a child, grew up in the same neighborhood with him, not knowing who he was and would become. I got to know him much later, after he assumed his bishopric. It was in the sixties that I started photographing him, not only in Kalwaria Zebrzydowska, but also at liturgy. When he became cardinal, I had to make an official portrait, which I had great trouble doing, because the Cardinal was at that time strangely unphotogenic. I had done many portraits of Cardinal Wyszynski before, but with Cardinal Wojtyla it never came off. Each picture was somehow not quite right. And then one day the Cardinal sat in an armchair in his apartment and said, "Now you can move me about as you wish. I give up." I started moving him closer and closer toward the window, and finally I got something passable. Nowadays these pictures are considered outstanding, but they were not very well received at the time.

In Poland, in Rome, and in the Vatican, I am called the Pope's photographer, but I do not bear that title, nor do I attempt to have it awarded to me. I think the reason I don't is that I continue the work started in Poland, the work of documenting the life of Karol Wojtyla. I don't make and don't have to make official photographs. The official photographers are Arturo Mari and Felici. The Felicis are a photographic clan who have had the privilege of photographing popes for about a hundred years and bear the title of *fotografo pontifice*. Their studio makes very high quality pictures. Arturo Mari, the official photographer for *L'Osservatore Romano*, has his studio in the Vatican. He would be the counterpart of the Polish Photographic Agency, that is, he has to document absolutely everything. If, for example, a high state or Church official visits the Pope, Mari takes pictures at every stage of the meeting, except, of course, for private talks. As for me, I can photograph things the others don't notice, because they have to work within a certain procedure. I am not bound by this procedure. I have much more freedom; I can take a picture of the Holy Father from the side or from the back; I can capture his expression, be it a frown or a smile.

When, at the very beginning of the pontificate, I saw the Holy Father saying his first Angelus to the enthusiastic crowds gathered outside the Vatican Palace, my eyes filled with tears of emotion, and I could not get the camera in focus. I thought to myself, "So that is it! Perhaps I shall go back to Krakow and continue making albums about my city, the surrounding landscape, about mysterious places, about Auschwitz; I will take up subjects that drew me to photography in the first place." And then a policeman came up to me and indicated that I was to follow him. (I don't know the Italian language very well, and at that time I didn't know it at all.) I thought I was being removed from the square. But the policeman led me through the palace corridors to a room where the Pope was receiving some dignitaries. Seeing me enter, the Holy Father smiled, and I knew he wanted me to stay and take the pictures.

Usually I select certain themes and then get them approved. I once took a large series of pictures of the Holy Father in the Castel Gandolfo gardens during his holiday rest. His walks in the olive garden seemed most beautiful to me. In some mysterious way, the white figure of the Pope summoned up images of biblical scenes.

I once rushed into the Vatican Palace out of breath. The Holy Father was very busy preparing for the visit of some high state official. The *valet de chambre* urged me to hurry, but my equipment wasn't ready yet. And then I heard the Pope's voice from inside the room, "Has Adam come yet?" So I picked up all my bits and pieces and entered the room. The Pope was already putting his pen back into his pocket. I said, "Holy Father, could you please hold on just a second!" He gave me an impish smile, took the cap off his pen, put it to paper, and asked, "Something like that?" That was a nice thing to do.

One day I was to take pictures at the Pope's summer residence. We were standing on the balcony. For some strange reason, I was very tense. The Pope sensed it and said, "Listen, we've got a session today. What should I put on?" And in that jocular fashion he defused my tension.

I usually come to Castel Gandolfo early in the morning. Once the Holy Father took me by the chin and said, "Eh! A beardless Bujak is no Bujak at all!" To which I replied, "But I shaved my beard ten years ago." "Yes, I remember, I remember!" Another time, when he was passing by me, he said, "Long live artistic photography!" On several occasions I was astonished by this intimacy, by his natural, friendly way of life.

But my Vatican life has its dark sides as well. One of them is my black suit, snow-white shirt, and polished shoes. They hinder my work because I feel best in casual clothes, when I don't have to remember to straighten my tie. This dog collar around my neck is the biggest pain. On one occasion I came to work dressed in my beautiful black suit, but I had a green bag on my shoulder. A friend of mine told me, "You are so finely dressed, but that green bag. . . ." So be it—the only thing to do was to go and buy a bag to suit the rest of my outfit.

I count the papal visits to hospitals in Rome among the most moving of my experiences. The Holy Father would stand on one side of the bed, I on the other, so that I could have an eye on the face and gestures of both the Pope and the patient. The following scene etched itself particularly deeply in my memory: A woman patient was lying motionless and looked as if dead. The Holy Father came up to her, stroked her face, and kissed her on the forehead. She opened her eyes and tried to raise her head in order to say something to him. The Holy Father bent over her and said some words I didn't understand. It was a moving spectacle. He approached each of the several hundred patients in the same manner, never missing a single person. His empathy in bowing down to the suffering confirmed my conviction that this is the Pope of Love.

I also photographed the Antonov trial, at which the key witness was Agca.

I had the good fortune to be present on the very day Agca was shown some hitherto unseen film footage, which had captured the moment shots had been fired at the Holy Father. Complete silence prevailed in the projection room. Agca was let out of the courtroom cage and seated some one-and-a-half meters from the TV monitor, on which we could at that moment see the assassin's hand, the trigger being pulled, and

the Holy Father collapsing. Although I was seething with emotion, I never took my eyes off Agca. I noticed that when the shot was being fired in the film, his leg jerked slightly. That was his only reaction during the entire screening.

Immediately afterward he was taken back to the cage. With trembling hands, I started taking pictures of him. I made a whole series of portraits that day.

One morning, I was ushered into the Pope's private chapel. The Pope had already been there, praying on his knees. The door closed behind me, and the two of us were alone in the chapel. Silence filled the room. Frossard once wrote that in prayer the Pope talks to God. And indeed, that was how I perceived him at that moment. He appeared to be mentally somewhere else. His hands moved up and down his face and forehead in that distinctive, slightly nervous manner. Those beautiful, unique hands were very eloquent. I wanted to preserve the image of those hands for posterity. I often do that. I started to unzip my bag very slowly, but I made a slight noise. The Holy Father turned in my direction, nodded his head to greet me, and resumed his prayers. I started taking photographs of him very unobtrusively, so as not to disturb him in his meditation.

I also photographed the Holy Father on Easter Thursday, when he performed the rite of washing the feet of twelve sick and handicapped persons. He did it with immense commitment and humility and bestowed a kiss on the feet of each of these suffering souls. I was deeply moved when I photographed these gestures. I am very often moved when I accompany the Holy Father, and sometimes tears blur my vision. I am always careful to hide my misty eyes behind the camera.

On Easter Saturday 1987, I was told to report immediately to the Vatican Palace. With prelate Stanislaw Dziwisz, I entered

an elevator, thinking that I was going to the Pope's quarters. But when the elevator door opened, it turned out that we were on the Palace terrace. Father Prelate, who had been accompanying me, said, "The Holy Father is supposed to be somewhere around." And so he was. Not long afterward I saw him performing the Stations of the Cross. He also saw me, waved his hand, and smiled. Then he kneeled down and continued his prayers. I put my eye to the viewfinder to capture the moment of prayer in the unlikely scenery of the terrace, above the rattle and hum of the city. Later I took some pictures of the dome of St. Peter's Basilica from that extraordinary location. Having finished the Stations of the Cross service, the Pope came out into the glass porch, recited the breviary, and then came up to me to talk. Then I made a whole series of portraits. When I was taking my leave, he asked me, "Are you going to Krakow?" The question was ringing with such longing and sadness that my heart was rent asunder.

It has been eleven years since I started my humble work at the side of the Holy Father. I has been a labor of love, devotion, and commitment. It has also been my prayer and wellspring of immense joy. I consider it a great privilege to be allowed so often by the side of Christ's Vicar, to see him at prayer and at work, to see him alone and meditating, but sometimes also brimming with joy. I am happy that, by documenting his service to the Church on film, I am able to bring his person and the hands that give their blessing to the entire world, closer to people.

Adam Bujak

The Church is an organic communion, in which
every person has his own place and his own task to fulfill.

Through the inscrutable will of the Almighty
I was called from this very land, from the site of the
martyrdom of St. Stanislaw, the royal city of Krakow,
to perform Peter's office.

The Church, inspired by the eschatological faith,
considers the stewardship of man, of his humanity,
of the future of people on earth, and of the direction of
man's development and progress as its inalienable duty.

The Church strives to serve the cause of unity
between people and nations. It is part of the
redemptive mission of the Church.

Only a person can give love
and only a person can receive it.

I feel this Polish solidarity,
solidarity of all my brothers and sisters
who speak the same language and bear the legacy
of a common historical experience.

To be a living branch in the vineyard of the Church means above all to be in living communion with the vine of Christ.

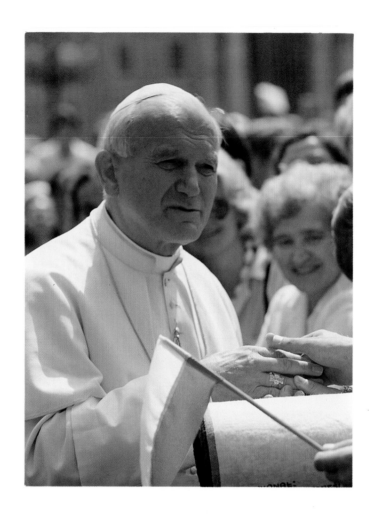

I have an acute awareness of what Poland is;
I bear in my heart especially the epoch to which we all
belong and which we are all creating.

. . . In the name of God's mission,
the Church becomes guardian of that freedom which
endows the human person with true dignity.

Through a genuine will to renounce sin
Christians should stand against the degradation of man;
through the testimony of their lives
they should profess the joy of emancipation from sin
through the redeeming grace of Christ.

Each of us has the duty to see that good is done
in his own life, in the life of his neighbors,
in the life of his society, in the life of the Church.
This responsibility is closely bound to prudence.

In modern civilization man is threatened with the disease of shallowness. We have to work toward retrieving the depth—the depth which defines the human person. The depth which poses a challenge to his mind and heart, a challenge not unlike the call of the sea. It is the depth of truth and freedom, of justice and love. The depth of peace.

From *Wszyscy z wszystkimi. Wszyscy dla wszystkich. Gdynia.*
Quotation from: "Do końca ich umilowal", p. 142.

Every day we have to redeem ourselves anew;
every day we have to find again that gift bestowed on us
by Christ when we took holy orders, by understanding the
redemptive mission of the Church and reflecting on the
enormous role our calling plays in that mission.

Merciful love in human relations
is never a one-sided act or process.

Man receives the merciful love of God
only as far as he transforms himself inwardly
in the spirit of such love in relation to others.

Man is called upon to enter into communion with God,
a friendship with God. God wants to be close to man.
God wants to confide His plans to man. He wants man to
partake of His life. He wants man to have God's joy.

**Blessed be all who have mercy
and may mercy be upon them, as our Lord said.**

Our civilization—especially Western civilization —based upon the development of science and technology, attaches great significance to intellectual and physical effort, but the spiritual struggle of man to give shape to his human self is no longer seen as important. As a result, a man who lives within the confines of our civilization often loses his sense of proportion and the inward sense of his own humanity. Both the effort to achieve this humanity and the joy of fulfillment—the joy of finding and meeting himself—are alien to him.

From *Pokuta pomaga odnaleźć się w prawdzie.*
Quotation from: *Jan Pawel II do Ludu Bożego*, p. 98.

Concern for moral order is inextricably bound
with the well-being of man and nation.

The Church has no other life than that endowed to her
by her Lord and Bridegroom.

Nowhere in the Gospel can either forgiveness or mercy,
which lie at its core, be taken to mean indulgence toward
depravation, suffering, or insult inflicted on a person.

The Gospel is directed to the weak, the poor, the meek and humble, the peacemaking, and the merciful, but it also continually calls upon us to be strong.

The young will never be strong
and the old will never keep their faith
if they have not learned to receive the Cross.

Everything depends on which way and to what extent
the parents and the family fulfill their first and foremost
task—how they will teach this being to be human
who, thanks to them, enjoys the gift of life.

Blessed be the hands, blessed be the hearts and minds
of all who minister to the sick.

Jesus Christ is the stable principle and fixed center of the mission that God Himself has entrusted to man. We must all share in this mission and concentrate all our forces on it, since it is more necessary than ever for modern mankind.

From *Redemptor hominis*, no. 11.

I open my heart to all Brethren
from Christian Churches and Communities. . . .

Christ does not wish for us to be hungry.
Christ does not wish for us to be hollow.
He wishes for us to find the spiritual nourishment of truth
and love at the Table of the Eucharist and God's Word.

The Church, which as God's People was founded
on the mystery of Incarnation and Redemption,
which is ever reborn in the Descent of the Holy Spirit,
this Church is a visible reality
with a strictly defined hierarchical order.

Man in the full truth of his existence, of his personal being and also of his community and social being—in the sphere of his own family, in the sphere of society and very diverse contexts, in the sphere of his own nation or people (perhaps still only that of his clan or tribe), and in the sphere of the whole of mankind—this man is the primary route that the Church must travel in fulfilling her mission: *he is the primary and fundamental way for the Church*, the way traced out by Christ Himself, the way that leads invariably through the mystery of the Incarnation and the Redemption.

From *Redemptor hominis*, no. 14.

Let the great family of ordained clergy
remain servants of God's People,
disciples of Him Who was faithful unto His death, of Him
Who came upon this world not to be served but to serve.

The Church professes in all humility that only the love
which is above the triviality of human differences may
bring to fruition this unity for which Christ prayed to His
Father and for which He still prays on our behalf in
supplications which words cannot express.

The Church shares with the people of our time
that deep, fervent desire for a life founded upon
the principle of justice.

. . . The institution of the University ranks among the masterpieces of human culture. We may wonder, though, if this masterpiece is not being counterfeited in our times. . . . The aim of a university is knowledge and wisdom. The aim of the Church is salvation, the Gospel, the order of love, and the supernatural order. Saint Thomas saw a clear division between the order of knowledge and the order of love. They are not identical—they are complementary.

From an address to the Catholic University in Lublin.
In *Jan Pawel II na Ziemi Polskiej*, pp. 166, 167.

Those who regard repentance as an expression of
the repressive mentality of the Church are mistaken.
The sacrament of confession represents not repression
but liberation, it does not aggravate guilt but destroys it;
it releases the burden of the perpetrated evil,
it gives the grace of forgiveness.

Repentance is not only an effort and a burden, but also joy.
Joy of spirit sometimes so powerful
as no other source can provide.

My great wish is that Poland never cease to be the country
of clerical callings and the land of great testimony to Christ.

The priesthood demands a special indivisibility
of life and ministry. This indivisibility lies at the very core
of our identity as ministers.

The history of a nation ought to be appraised
according to its contribution to the progress of man, of
his awareness, compassion, and conscience, as these
faculties are the foundation, the essence, and the
source of the power of culture.

From an address at the Victory Square in Warsaw.
In *Gaude Mater Polonia*, p. 26.

Without prayer, the lifestyle of a priest is warped.

Only through prayer can we ensure that . . . great tasks
and mounting obstacles do not lead to a crisis,
but provide an opportunity and, in a sense, the source
for more and more mature achievements
in the march of God's People to the Promised Land
at the close of the second millennium.

The more the ministry of the Church is focused on man,
the more, shall we say, "anthropocentric" it is,
the more it needs to be theocentric,
that is, directed toward the Father.

The Apostolic See is happy to welcome diplomatic
representatives not only as spokesmen for their
governments and political systems and structures,
but also as representatives of nations, which in these
structures realize their sovereignty and their political right
of self-determination, whether these societies are
numerically big or small.

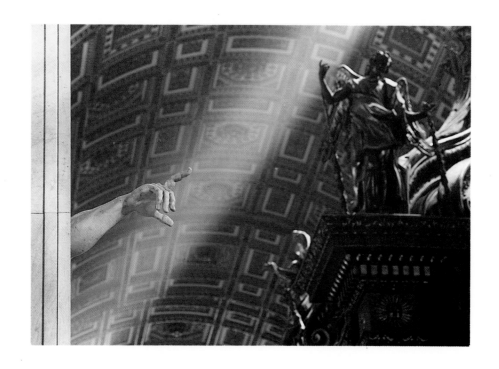

The Church operates within the realm
of the Mystery of Redemption, which has become
the most fundamental principle of her life and ministry.

Hail to You, the Cross, wherever you are, in the fields,
by the roadside, in places where people suffer and die . . .
where they work, study, and create. . . .

One has to delve deep into the mystery of Christ's Offering
in order to draw inspiration for daily ministry
toward those who need our charity, the ministry of the
Church and all people of good will.

The workplace is for the home, because the home is for
man. The home is for man, and labor is for man. Man ought
to have his home through labor, and through labor man
ought to grow in his human home.

In order to serve others skillfully and efficiently
one ought to have self-control
and virtues which allow this self-control.

To be a Christian is to be on a constant vigil. As the soldier
who stands guard is on a vigil, as a mother is on a vigil by
her child, as a physician is on a vigil by the patient's bed.
To be on a vigil is to protect the value of good.

There is a beautiful custom in Rome that each Sunday and
holy day the Pope says the Angelus with the faithful who
gather at St. Peter's Square for that purpose.
This custom is the legacy of my Honorable Predecessors,
above all Paul VI, and I am happy to cherish it.

We are with you who suffer poverty and hunger, who often witness the dying of your own children crying out for a piece of bread;

we are with you millions of refugees exiled from your own homes and countries;

we are with you victims of terror, locked in prisons and concentration camps, destroyed by cruelty and torture;

we are with you who were kidnapped;

we are with you whose daily life is marred by the threat of violence and civil war;

we are with you who suffer from unpredictable natural disasters . . . ;

we are with you, the families who pay for their Christian faith the price of discrimination, whose children are barred from education and professional careers;

we are with you, the parents who are mortified because of the spiritual anguish and sense of loss in your children;

we are with you young people who are despondent because you cannot find a job, a home, and a place in the society, and may not enjoy the attendant dignity;

we are with you who suffer from sickness, old age, or loneliness;

we are with you who grope in the dark of anxiety and doubt and cry out for illumination of mind and peace of heart;

we are with you who, bowing under the burden of your sins, cry out for the mercy of Christ the Redeemer.

In *Krzyż znakiem naszej wiary i nadziei*, pp. 179–180.

It is crucial that every member of the community
of God's People not only "belongs socially",
but also has a specific avocation.

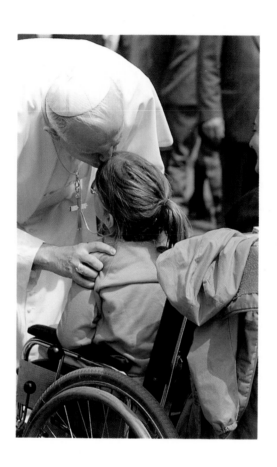

We must bow down to and honor those brothers and sisters
who are weak and helpless, deprived of something we are
provided with, which we enjoy every day.

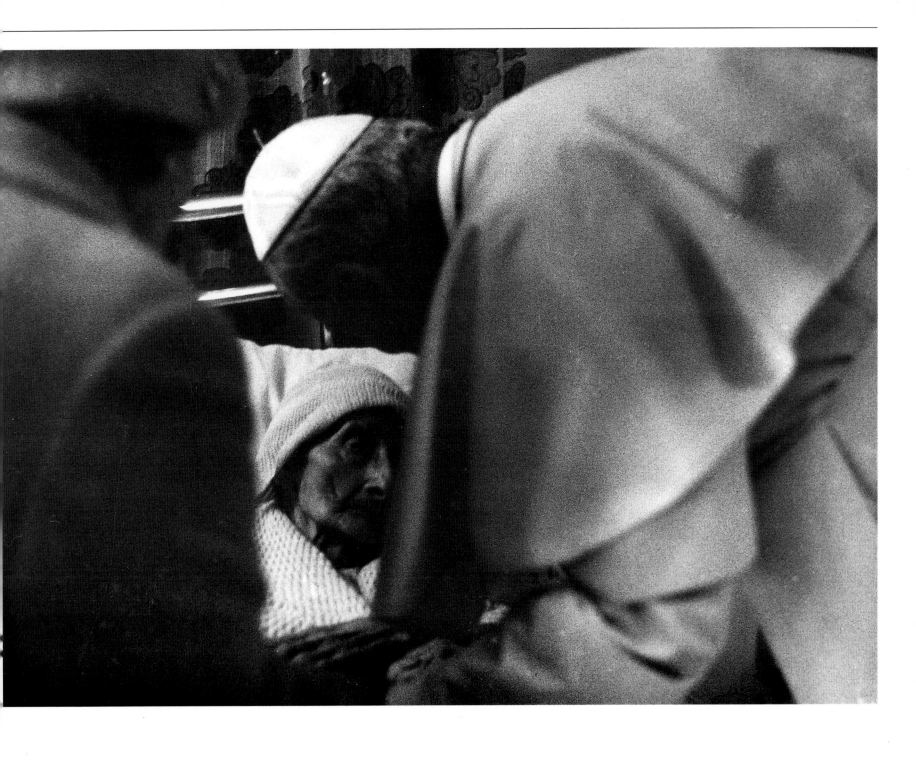

The sick and the old, the handicapped and those
in need of care, they make us acutely aware
how much we have to rely on each other
and how close to each other we are.

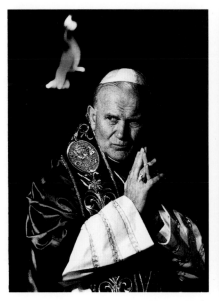

In order to understand the meaning of suffering, we should look not so much at the sinner but at Jesus Christ, his Redeemer. The Son of God, Who did not deserve His suffering and Who could have avoided it, chose to follow the path of suffering to its very end out of love for man.

Hail to You, Cross of Christ! Wherever is your sign,
Christ bears witness to His passover, His "transition from
death to life", and bears witness to love, which is the
life-force, which overcomes death.

The Cross of Christ is a great revelation of the meaning of suffering, its value in human life and in history. He who understands the Cross, who embraces it, enters the path on which he will not struggle with or contest God, but ascend to Him along the path of Christ, the Way of the Cross, the Via Crucis.

General audience, March 30, 1982.
In *Krzyż znakiem naszej wiary i nadziei*, p. 69 (1).

The messianic program of Christ—the program of
mercy—has become the program of His people, the program
of the Church. The Cross will always be at the center of this
program because the revelation of merciful love achieves in
it its most intense expression.

May the resurrected Christ inspire all Christians and
non-Christians with feelings of solidarity and merciful love
toward all our brethren who are in need.

Culture is the expression of man. It is the confirmation of his humanity. Man creates it and through it he creates himself. He creates himself through the inward effort of spirit: mind, will, and heart. But man also creates culture in community with others. Culture is the expression of human communication, common thinking, and cooperation. It serves the common good and becomes the common good of human communities.

From a speech to young people, Gniezno.
In *Przemówienia: Homilie*, p. 54.

I address . . . all men—and each man—and with what reverence an apostle of Jesus Christ has to pronounce this word: man! Pray for me! Help me, so I can serve you!

From the inaugural address.
In *Jan Pawel II do Ludu Bożego*, p. 1.

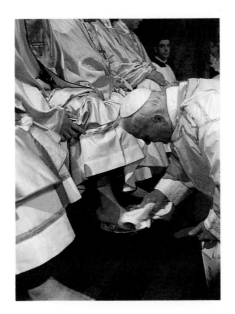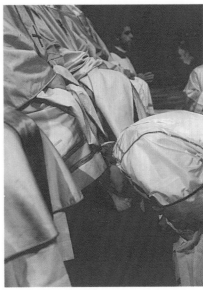

Christ feels the need to lower Himself to the feet
of His Apostles, and this tells us so much about Him.
Will He not, by giving Himself away in the Eucharist,
forever lower Himself to the level of so many human hearts?
Will He not be forever ministering to them?

May the world be able to enjoy peace,
may Europe be able to enjoy peace and stability,
may my Homeland be able to enjoy peace and respect for its
right to exist among the nations of Europe and the world.

Prayer is the path of the Word, which embraces all.
The path of the Primordial Word that renders
unto the Holy Father all which is of Him.

If . . . we want to have an adequate picture of the
multitudinous and diversified community of God's People,
we must above all see Christ, Who in one way or another
says to every member of that community, "Follow Me".

It is you, Peter, who wishes to be the paving here,
so they tread upon you (not knowing where they go)
and go whither you direct their steps. . . .

To be a living vine in the vineyard of the Church means also
to take upon oneself responsibilities in the community of
the Church and in society.

Only he who accepts the limits of his reason and his moral
weakness, who accepts the need of salvation, may open
himself up to faith and in faith meet his Redeemer in Christ.

In its proper and full meaning, mercy is not identical with even the most discerning and most sympathetic view of moral, physical, or material evil. In its proper and full manifestation, mercy reveals itself as lifting up, as dragging up of good from under layers of evil which exist in the world and in man. In this sense, mercy constitutes the central part of the messianic message of Christ and the primary force of His ministry.

From *Bożym Milosierdziu*, p. 34.

The Eucharist not only bears witness
to Him Whose "love knew no bounds".
The Eucharist is also the school of such love.

The Eucharist is bound to the earth.
The bread and wine which we bring into it
are symbols of the gifts of the earth,
gifts of the Creator, and fruit of man's labor.

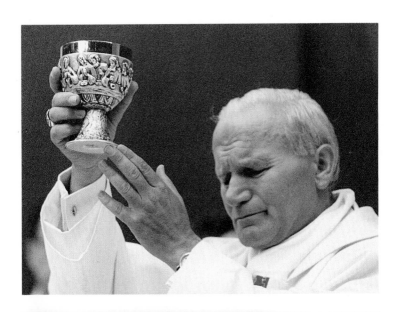

The Eucharist can be given out by us only through service!

Man is afraid, and justly so, that he may fall victim to pressure which will deprive him of inward dignity, the right to speak the truth of which he is convinced, the faith he professes, and the right to listen to the voice of his conscience, which guides him in his moral choices. The technical means which our civilization has developed can lead not only to its self-destruction through military conflict, but also to "peaceful" subjugation of individuals, communities, and entire societies and nations which for some reason stand in the way of those who have these means at their disposal and would not shrink from using them.

In *Bożym Miłosierdziu*, p. 56 (5).

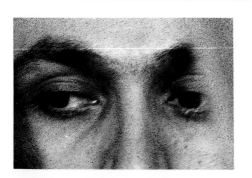

Through my own experience I felt a particular affinity
to all those who in any place on this earth and in any way
suffer persecution for their Christian faith.
And to all those who are repressed
for promoting the holy cause of man and his dignity.

Man often seems to overlook other uses of the natural
environment than exploiting it to meet his current needs.
But the Creator wanted man to serve as a prudent and noble
"master" and "steward" of nature, not a ruthless "exploiter".

Man is ennobled by God, Who called him into being,
accepted him, and is leading him toward perfection.

The Church rejoices when anywhere in the world, in any country or society, creative urges of every individual are recognized, when space for realizing these urges is created.

Christ answers even the deepest desires of the human being.
The desire for love is one of them.
And He is the One Whose "love knew no bounds".

The personality of the priest must be
a clear model and signpost for others
It is the essential precondition of our pastoral ministry.

Labor is . . . the fundamental dimension of human earthly existence. It has not only technical but also ethical significance for man. Man is "master" of the earth only as much as he is a master and not a slave of labor. Labor should help man become better, spiritually more mature, more responsible, help him to fulfill his human calling both as an individual and as a member of a community, and above all, as a member of the basic human community, the family.

Address to pilgrims from Upper Silesia, Czestochowa.
In *Przemówienia: Homilie*, p. 164.

Man cannot be truly free but through love,
the supreme love of God and the love of men, brethren,
neighbors, countrymen. . . . This is what Christ, whose love
knew no bounds, teaches us. This is what the Eucharist,
the holiest legacy of God's foster children, tells us.

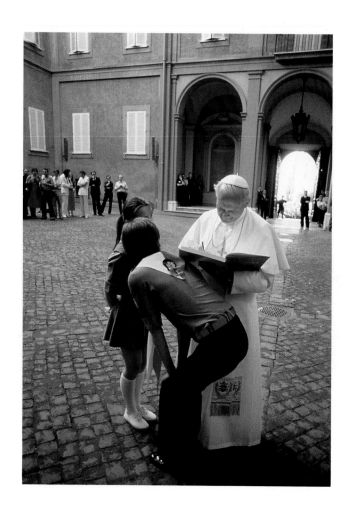

Merciful love is particularly indispensable
in relationships between the closest of kin,
between spouses, between parents and children;
it is indispensable in education and ministry.

It is my deepest desire that all followers of Christ
in my country never cease to discover brotherhood
in Christ, which springs from common baptism.

Prayer should embrace all that makes up our life.
It cannot be a supplement or an aside.
Everything should find its expression in prayer.

The moral strength of the woman, her spiritual power,
is connected with the awareness that God entrusted her
with a special responsibility for man.

It is a noble thing to have a predisposition for understanding every person, analyzing every system and recognizing what is right; this does not at all mean losing certitude about one's own faith or weakening the principles of morality, the lack of which will soon make itself felt in the life of whole societies, with deplorable consequences besides.

From *Redemptor hominis*, no. 6.

Prayer helps us maintain our faith, trust, and love even
when our human weakness would destroy them.

The image of the Virgin from Jasna Gora has become
the symbol of spiritual unity for Poles around the world.
It is also a badge of our spirituality, of our place
in the huge family of Christian peoples
brought together in the unity of the Christ.

The Church has always taught the duty to act for the common good and, in so doing, has likewise educated good citizens for each state. Furthermore, she has always taught that the fundamental duty of power is solicitude for the common good of society; this is what gives power its fundamental rights. Precisely in the name of these premises of the objective ethical order, the rights of power can only be understood on the basis of respect for the objective and inviolable rights of man. The common good that authority in the state serves is brought to full realization only when all the citizens are sure of their rights.

From *Redemptor hominis*, no. 17.

The last night of awaiting the Savior, of which the liturgy
of the Church reminds us through Christmas Eve and
Christmas Day, is at the same time the night of fulfillment.
Born is He Who was awaited, Who was and never ceases
to be the aim of the Advent of humanity. Christ is born.

Prayer allows us to be continually redeemed,
to strive continually toward God,
which is necessary if we are to lead others unto God.

The Cross means to give your life for your brother to save your own life through saving his.

The Cross means that love prevails over hate and revenge—that it is better to give than to take, that acting is more efficient than demanding.

The Cross means that there is no shipwreck without hope, no darkness without a star, no storm without a safe haven.

The Cross means that love knows no bounds: start with those who are closest to you, and do not forget those who are farthest from you.

The Cross means that God is greater than we humans, who are fallible; that He is our salvation in the biggest calamity; and that life prevails over death.

From an address during the European Vespers on Heldenplatz in Vienna.
In *Krzyż znakiem naszej wiary i nadziei*, p. 86.

Do not forget me in your prayers. On Jasna Gora
and around the entire country. May this Pope,
who is blood of your blood and heart of your hearts,
serve well the Church and the world in the difficult era
when the second millennium is coming to a close.